I0797373

ATTICUS

BEST *of* POETRY

Poems, Epigrams & Aphorisms

Atticus Publishing
2220 Colorado Avenue
Santa Monica, California 90404
United States
www.atticuspoetry.com

ISBN: 979-8-218-17106-3

Editor: Duncan Penn
Art Director: Ashley Chase
Designer: Marissa Campeau
Production Manager: Ashley Chase

Also by Atticus

LVOE.
The Truth About Magic
The Dark Between Stars
Leave Her Wild

To you,

Ten years ago, almost to the day of writing this, I met a man in France. We became close friends and he shared with me how writing poetry had saved his life. It was a thought that never left me. A few days later, while walking the streets of Paris, I wrote my very first poem. Little did I know, it would change me forever and—in all ways that matter—would save my life.

Through these simple poems, I have found solace in desperate times, comfort in uncertainty, and purpose in chaos. I am humbled and deeply grateful for you and the opportunity to share these words with you; whether you have been with me for years, days, or minutes, it's a pleasure to be together now.

I believe, your presence is a testament to the transformative healing power of poetry and the enduring human yearning for connection, love, and expression. It is no mistake you're here, for as they say, poetry finds you exactly when it needs to.

So cheers to you and a decade of writing simple words on simple pages, and hopefully to a lifetime more.

I hope one of these pages makes a moment a little better for you or, better yet, inspires you to take a chance as I did and uncover the words, colors, and art living within you.

Until then, from the bottom of my heart, thank you... for saving my life!

xx
Atticus

We aspire
only to live
our lives well,
to fall into the gentle to and fro of life,
and the refrains of seasons and tides
rocking us slowly & finally to sleep
as old and loved
as we can possibly be.

Some moments
like some people
are not meant
to be fully understood
so for now
it's best
we just call them miracles.

The way he talked of their dreams
it made her want to grab his hand
and run quickly into their tomorrows.

There will always be that moment
when we look at someone
for the first time in love with them.

The day I met you I began
to forget a life without you.

Love
is diving headfirst
into someone else's confusion and finding
that it all makes sense.

You will never be unloved by me
you are well too tangled in my soul.

"I love you more than chocolate," she said.
And I just wasn't ready
for that sort of pressure.

We were
endlessly
carelessly
hopelessly
in love
and the rest
was just the details.

My

atoms

love

your

atoms,

it's

chemistry.

People will say you're beautiful
but it takes a special person
to make you believe it.

Love exists
somewhere between
a girl pretending
she can't open a jar of pickles
and a boy pretending
not to know she could.

BEST of POETRY
ATTICUS

"When do I know
if I really love her?"
asked the boy
and the old man smiled,
"When it's no longer
a question."

Be yourself.
Someone out there loves
the person
you're pretending not to be.

Hurry up,
she said— let's grow old together.

To love and be loved is the true poetry of life.

You are
the series of mistakes
that needed to happen
for you to find your you.

All she wanted
was that cozy love
the kind that felt like
hot chocolate,
rainstorms
or wood fires
in small houses
hard to describe
but you know it when you got it.

I won't ever find the words for you—
you are my everything always
and even that is not enough.

Finding her
was remembering her
from a thousand
different dreams.

Never
neglect
a kiss
or a sunset.

She tore poems
from my flesh,
in fights,
in love,
and sex.

The truth about magic
lies in the very
perfect fading wish
of every shooting star.

I loved you once
in a swimming pool in France
it was summer and it rained
I looked at you
and loved you then
I never told you
but it's true
I loved you
and us
and the chance of all things
and even though
it didn't last
I will always love
that day I loved you.

BEST of POETRY
ATTICUS

Don't waste
a second
of your time
convincing
other people
you're worth
loving.

I want to be with someone
who dreams of doing everything in life, and nothing
on a rainy Sunday afternoon.

You and I
are stars
met once
in the breath of a universe
crossed only for a moment
as the ebb and flow
of dust and atoms.

She was incandescently beautiful
and beauty was the least of her.

You are worth your imperfections
you are worth your bad days
you are worth your good
you are worth your confusion
you are worth your insecurities
you are worth fighting for
and you are worth loving.
And that's a fck'ing fact.

We were strange in love
her and I
too wild to last,
too rare to die.

Our lovers fascinate us—
we live in perpetual awe
of the particular way they are.

Write about me
she said—
for what's the use
in loving a poet
if they don't
make you
live forever.

"I don't know many things
with any certainty,"
she said,
"but snuggling feels important."

To be alive
is the strange
and wondrous miracle
we forget.

She has him always in her closed eyes.

You weren't given wings
to see the world from a tree.

BEST *of* POETRY
ATTICUS

True love comes
when you lose
where you end
and they begin
and the atoms
in your souls
forget where they belong
and slowly you become
pieces of each other
too close now
to ever be apart.

How dare you
dare me
to dare
fall in love with you.

"I don't believe in magic,"
the young boy said.
And the old man smiled,
"You will, when you see her."

Every moment spent with her
I become a little more sure
anything is possible.

I promised
to kiss her
a million times
before I died,
fifty a day
for the rest of my life—
so when I was gone
she could smile
knowing
there wasn't a place
on her I missed.

What if you were already
the incredible person
you're pretty sure you could be?

It's always safe
to do nothing
when it rains.

"Silly girl,"
the old lady laughed,
"your
different
is
your
beautiful."

In the right love

we will discover new love for ourselves.

She burrowed her face
into me.
"I missed you,"
she said,
"long before I ever knew you."

Love
waits for all of us
quietly
in that place
where no one
is looking.

There is all sorts of magic
beaming in your bones.

BEST *of* POETRY

Don't waste any more tomorrows
on someone who wastes your todays.

True love exists in moments
stumbled upon
by accident
in hospitals
in airports
and underneath the stars
gone before you realize it was there
missed before you knew you had it.

No great love
was perfect,
no great love
wasn't bravely
fought for you.

I will follow you,
my love,
to the edge of all our days,
to our very last
tomorrows.

Her courage was her crown
and she wore it like a queen.

And the stars blinked
as they watched her carefully
jealous of the way she shone.

We just want
the world to love
the little monsters
that we are.

Never
be afraid
to change
the prince's name
in your
story.

When I saw you first, it took
every ounce of me not to kiss you.
When I saw you laugh, it took
every ounce of me not to love you.
And when I saw your soul, it took every ounce of me.

Break my heart
and you will find yourself inside.

If I'm being honest
it was a disturbingly short
amount of time
between meeting you
and wanting to say
"I love you."

I feel
like girls
who drink
whiskey
tell
good
stories.

BEST of POETRY
ATTICUS

Imagine we all had the courage to be
the strange
and wondrous creatures
we were born to be.

You are
enough,
a thousand
times
enough.

I lost my way
all the way to you
and in you
I found
all the way
back
to me.

Have you ever looked at the stars drunk
and sworn they were burning just for you?
It's hard not to believe in magic
it's hard not to believe in whiskey.

We fall in love
with the little things
somebody loves
about the world
like music,
rainy days,
or peanut butter sandwiches—
and it doesn't matter
what they are,
it's just that they love them
and that makes us happy.

I live
my life
so
happily
in
crazy
with
her.

Twice
I would die
for a little more
once once once
with you.

Love
by its very nature
is fragile
and that's what makes
true love
so powerful—
you make a fragile
thing
strong.

Love is
late-night
kissing at stoplights
after the lights
have turned green.

I woke before her
and she slept on as the sun rose
spilling light across our bed
she was an angel in my sheets
the girl I would draw
if given a thousand years
and only a promise
she might one day come to life.

She was that wild thing I loved.
My dark between the stars.

Smile
and let go
it's just life after all
and you're doing
it right
just by living.

ATTICUS

The boy ran
quick as rain
through grassy fields awake in dew
in moon-dipped steps
a summer's night
through fireflies
and sparkling stars
a glass jar in hand
his little cloud breaths
up to the open sky.
And
there at once
alone in that summer field, she flew
a fairy shining
as bright as day
and the stars, once bright
dimmed back in crimsons
jealous of the way she shone
she, the brightest light he'd ever seen
so bright she burned, for she loved him too
and he put her gently in his hands
and placed her in the jar
his love
within his coat.
Back to the town, he ran
a thousand laughs caught in his throat
everything he loved

was finally his
and there, with all the people's eyes around
he brought the jar out from his robes
and held it high above
his shining prize
for all to see.
but, alas
she was dim
and though she tried
she could not shine so brightly
and the boy's heart fell
and the people turned away and laughed.
"But I love her," he said.
"More than anything I could ever love.
Why can't she shine for the world?"
And the old man in the corner
beckoned the boy close
to whisper something in his car.
The boy looked up and back at his fairy.
dimming in the glass.
He nodded at the man
for he knew the old man's words were true
and with tears in his eyes
sparkling like diamonds he ran
faster than he'd ever run
the wind tearing his eyes ever more back
through the moonlit steps

through the darkened grass
through the fireflies
and shimmering stars and
there
in that summer field, alone
he opened up the glass once more
and held it to the sky
and his love, his fairy, flittered out tenderly,
brightly
she began to burn again
even brighter than before
and as he cried
and loved her so
the old man's words
echoed in his mind
love
her
he said
but leave her wild.

You feel right
to me, she said,
like naked
on cashmere.

Love is a wondrous and wild
storm
we must—
while we can—
dance in the rain.

Everything that was
and is
and ever will be
is within you.

It's too sunny today.
I just need you, some blankets and a storm.

You and I
will be
lost and found
a thousand times
along this
cobbled
road of us.

So often
we find in love
all the things
we never realized
we were searching for.

Chase your stars fool, life is short.

We are human
bold & brilliant
and we will rise always
from the ashes of our doubt
to wield our differences
not as a weakness
but as swords
to take our beauty back.

She didn't want love,
she wanted to be loved—
and that
was entirely different.

BEST of POETRY
ATTICUS

I have noticed
that in every photo
taken of us
we are either kissing
or about to
and I think that's
a beautiful truth about us.

"There's too much risk in loving," the young boy said.
"No,"
said the old man,
"There's too much risk in not."

If love could have saved us
we would have lived forever.

There are
magnets in my bones
for the iron
in her blood.

That was her magic—
she could still
see the sunset
even on those
darkest days.

She wasn't waiting for a knight—
she was waiting for a sword.

A thousand times
a day
I love you
a little more
than I did
the day before.

There is no safer place I know than
tucked
in a corner
of a café in Paris
with a bottle of rosé
and an afternoon to spare.

You are all the ways
my soul likes to dream.

If I'm honest,
very little in life
has compared
in immensity
or magnitude
before or since
to the electric
and wild feeling
of the first time
I kissed
a girl.

I think it's beautiful
the way you sparkle
when you talk about
the things you love.

Love
could
be
labeled
poison
and we'd
drink
it
anyways.

BEST of PO
ATTICUS

Never go in search of love
go in search of life
and life will find you
the love you seek.

Travel and love
are worth the sacrifice
for a life without them
is a life unexplored.

You set aflame
in my heart and mind
the most beautiful chaos.

She walked
through her life
tired
from the
mighty wings
upon her back.

My darling,
let's you and I
ramble on this life
awhile—
our hands in hands
our hearts in hearts
our shadows forever one.

A few drinks and the world was hers —
she wore her whiskey like a loaded gun.

I'm powerless
to write
of the beauty
that I see
in the curl
of her lips
when she smiles
while she sleeps.

"Do you hear that?"
he said,
"Listen close
the universe is singing to us
in shooting stars
daring us to fall in love."

It's always been him
she smiled
our souls just dance the same.

Young love is about loving the ones who leave you
old love is about loving the ones who never would.

She was no one
to me
on a train in May
and everyone
to me
under the stars in June.

He traced
her silhouette
with moonlight
and found in the stars
the calligraphy
of her soul.

BEST *of* POETRY
ATTICUS

A sky full of stars
and he was staring at her.

I race to fall asleep with you
to meet you
in the morning
a little more in love each day.

I love those laughs
that come from deep within
the kind that are catching to anyone close
that make your stomach hurt
and cry with tears of joy
the kind that come
when you least expect
where the more you try to stop
the harder it becomes
and even when you think of them now
you smile—
those are the laughs
of real old
human magic.

How beautiful you are,
he said,
a tapestry of scars.

One of those forever kinds of friends
where anything can happen
and nothing will change—
they just always are
and forever will be.

Watch carefully
the magic that occurs
when you give a person
enough comfort
to just be themselves.

The simplest truth
is that we
fall in love with the way someone
makes us feel or doesn't
and that's pretty well
the all of it.

Let's stop
pretending
to be so perfect
for the world
and get on
with finding out
if we can be
so perfect
for each other.

Broken flowers bloom the brightest.

I love you
he said
to the end of all things
and on—
and she smiled
soaking
in the infiniteness
of it all.

I'm glad I found you
because
before you
I never knew what to wish for.

Come on darling
she said
let's drink wine
and paint
our universe.

BEST of POETRY
ATTICUS

I fell in love
with
that strange
world
she was.

The sex was a bonus
to the great and wondrous privilege
of being in close proximity
to her jokes.

It was never the way she looked
always the way she was
I would have fallen in love with her
with my eyes closed.

The answer
to the question
"Are you in love?"
should be simple
and if it's not
then it is.

A soul mate would be great,
but at some point
I'd settle for someone who gets back to text messages.

I find more love
in a storm
with you
than a thousand
sunny days without.

That was her gift—
she filled you with words
you didn't know were there.

We all wear scars—
find someone
who makes yours
feel beautiful.

She was powerful
not because she wasn't scared
but because
she went on so strongly
despite the fear.

I will never be perfect for you
but I will always imperfectly try to be.

We are all worth loving
sometimes we just need
someone to take a chance on us.

The world slowed its spin
in awe of love
like cars slowing for an accident but instead of a fire
there was just you and I
kissing on a bridge in June.

BEST *of* POETRY

Your sweet laugh
wanders through
my mind
tiptoeing whispers
for my heart to find.

Her love
happened to me a hundred times at once,
in a thousand different ways
as a million different colors.

There is a great miracle
that occurs when we listen
to that little voice inside our heads
that tells us truthfully
who we are and why.

I needed to paint her
grab colors with my hands
and throw them at the wall
There I would yell
"This is my love for you!'

Love
the one they are
not the one
they should be.

She was one of the rare ones
so effortlessly herself
and the world loved her for it.

You have robbed me
of all heart & mind
and I love you
sweet bandit of my soul.

I wanted love
but not just any love
someone to look into my eyes
and see the truth of me
witness my pain
but also my hope
hold my soul
and never let go—
I wanted that love
and no other love
would do.

I want to know every part of you,
every scar,
every bruise,
I want to trace the map of you,
my fingers a compass,
your freckles the constellations
which in my heart I will chart
so when I close my eyes
I'll have you in my stars forever.

I loved her so intensely
words seemed unfit.

It was
her
chaos
that
made
her
beautiful.

“Your sweater smells like you,”
she said.
“I wish it were a magic sweater
so when I took it off
and shook it
you would arrive into it
just like magic—
I hate sweaters that aren’t magic.”

BEST of POETRY
ATTICUS

Across a room
tangled in her
imagination
they had spent
a lifetime together
before
he said
hello.

There is a moment
in some girls' lives
when they put on a dress
for the very first time
and walk into the world
feeling more beautiful
than thev ever have
and ever will again.

I love you most in that place
between coffee and sleep.

Love is not something to be found
it is something to be built
brick by careful brick
and the more carefully
it is built
the stronger it will be
for when life's winds blow
and storms shake the walls.

Love someone
like it's your very first night together
or your very last.

She was the dream
I had been searching for,
the one to
wake me up.

Our minds follow
well behind
the old magic of our souls that knows it's
in love
from the first moment
we see them.

I aspire to be
an old man
with an old wife
laughing at old jokes
from a wild youth.

We've moved on now
but if
I'm honest
I am still
a little bit
in love
with all the ways
we were.

And somewhere—
I like to think—
Audrey Hepburn smiles.

In all probability
there is a person out there
that is almost exactly the same
as the one you just lost,
except that they are a little bit taller,
a little bit kinder,
and a whole lot better in bed.

Don’t worry—
you see,
to some you are
magic.

BEST *of* POETRY
ATTICUS

An open window in Paris
is all the world I need.

Come, my darling,
it is never too late
to begin
our love again.

All I dream
is for our shadows
to spend
a little
more forever
together.

"What if she says no?"
asked the boy,
and the old man smiled,
"best not live scared of thorns
or you'll never find a rose."

The beautiful thing
about young love
is the truth
in our hearts that it will last forever.

I'm tired
of
their stories
let's write
our own.

Atticus